Follow Your Breath!

A First Book of Mindfulness

Scot Ritchie

Kids Can Press

Thank you, Julia Naimska, for years of patience, brilliant design and being in the moment — S.R.

Kids Can Press gratefully acknowledges the financial support of the Government of Ontario, through Ontario Creates; the Ontario Arts Council; the Canada Council for the Arts; and the Government of Canada for our publishing activity.

Published in Canada and the U.S. by Kids Can Press Ltd.
25 Dockside Drive, Toronto, ON M5A 0B5

Kids Can Press is a Corus Entertainment Inc. company

www.kidscanpress.com

The artwork in this book was rendered digitally.
The text is set in Futura.

Edited by Jennifer Stokes
Designed by Julia Naimska

Printed and bound in Shenzhen, China, in 5/2020
by C & C Offset

CM 20 0 9 8 7 6 5 4 3 2 1

Library and Archives Canada Cataloguing in Publication

Title: Follow your breath! : a first book of mindfulness / Scot Ritchie.
Names: Ritchie, Scot, author, illustrator.
Series: Ritchie, Scot. Exploring our community.
Description: Series statement: Exploring our community
Identifiers: Canadiana 20190204788 | ISBN 9781525303364 (hardcover)
Subjects: LCSH: Mindfulness (Psychology) — Juvenile literature.
Classification: LCC BF637.M56 R58 2020 | DDC j158.1/3 — dc23

Contents

Move to Mindful

The five friends are at Pedro's for a sleepover. Pedro is feeling anxious because he's moving in a few days. He's sad about leaving the house he grew up in — and worried he won't feel at home in his new house.

Pedro's mom is going to teach the friends about mindfulness. She thinks it might help Pedro feel better.

Mindfulness is noticing what is happening right now, in this moment. Practicing mindfulness means worrying less about past or future moments. Just like eating nutritious foods and exercising, being mindful is a way to take care of yourself.

4

Think and Do

Pedro's mom has lots of books on mindfulness. Sally also suggests they research online.

"There are useful websites and some really good apps," says Mrs. Rivera.

The friends learn that many people use mindfulness, including athletes, scientists, musicians — and even kids! In a busy, stressful world, mindfulness allows you to be still and pay attention to the moment. And when you do that, you feel more prepared to face the world!

Notice Your Body

The friends head to the community center, where Pedro's mom is leading a tae kwon do class. She invites the kids to do stretches as the class finishes. She also suggests they all walk to the park afterward.

"Good idea," says Yulee. "Nature and mindfulness go together."

Mindfulness is being aware of your mind *and* your body. Using your body is one of the best ways to practice mindfulness. Like most things, the more you practice, the better you get!

Feel the muscle you are stretching.

Stretch and Release

1. Close your eyes and gently bend forward. Let your arms hang loosely.

2. Breathe in through your nose and out through your mouth.

3. Feel your muscles stretch as your arms dangle. Feel how heavy your head is.

4. Hold this position for five slow breaths, then slowly stand up.

5. Notice your body. Does it feel different?

Focus!

Another way to be mindful is through meditation. But that doesn't have to mean sitting cross-legged on the ground! The friends are going on a mindful walk, but soon realize they need to go somewhere quieter than the park.

There are a lot of things you already do that are mindful — like walking! Or have you ever stopped to look at a ladybug on a leaf? When you are very focused on something, you're being mindful. Mindfulness is a simple idea, but it's not easy to do. Focusing on only one thing takes practice.

Your Nose Knows!

At the garden, the kids play a game using the sense of smell. First, each friend finds a rose and, with eyes closed, breathes in deeply through the nose, smelling the beautiful flower.

"Now, breathe out slowly through your mouth," says Mrs. Rivera.

Breathing slowly helps to bring the kids into the moment. After a few deep breaths, they're ready. Mrs. Rivera puts a raspberry in each of their hands.

When you close your eyes, your other senses become sharper. You can focus on smell when you're not distracted by what you're seeing. You can do this with all your senses. Try closing your eyes and listening.

Listen to the Bees

You Are Not Your Feelings

It's raining! This isn't what the friends expected, and they're upset. Martin reminds everyone that being mindful means paying attention to your feelings.

"My teacher says ignoring bad feelings can make you feel worse," says Pedro.

Like the weather, feelings change and are often beyond our control. If you feel sad or angry, try to notice and accept the feeling — without trying to change it. Feelings often drift away, just like clouds in the sky.

Through the Rain

It's hard not to let the rain spoil their day. Mrs. Rivera reminds the friends that being mindful will help them to accept the present moment instead of letting negative thoughts block the way.

"A bird gets wet when it flies through the rain," says Mrs. Rivera, "but that doesn't stop it from going where it wants to go."

Mindfulness can help us through difficult moments. Try letting go of your negative thoughts. How does it feel?

Nature on My Mind

The friends head back to Pedro's house. It's time for dinner, and everyone is hungry. But what's Sally doing? She stopped to notice how fresh everything smells in the rain. She is being mindful. Pedro isn't feeling quite as mindful!

Just being in nature can calm us. When we focus on the sights, smells and sounds of nature, things that worry us can be pushed aside. We can pay attention to what is happening in the moment.

Be There, Be Aware!

During dinner, Martin suggests everyone continue the mindfulness game they were playing in the garden, only this time with the sense of taste. The friends enjoy their dinner while chewing more slowly, experiencing each bite.

Being mindful means doing one thing at a time. If you're eating, just eat. Don't play with your toys or watch TV. Also, be aware if you are hungry or just eating out of habit or boredom.

Breathe Deep and Sleep

It's time for bed, and Pedro's mom has a surprise. She's going to teach the friends how to do a body scan. This can be done anytime, but it is a great way to calm down before bed.

Breathing is the most important thing to notice when you're being mindful. Your breath is always there, and you can rely on it. It helps you to stay present. Rest your hands on your belly and feel your belly rise and fall with each breath. Imagine a boat on waves. As you slow your breathing, the waves calm down.

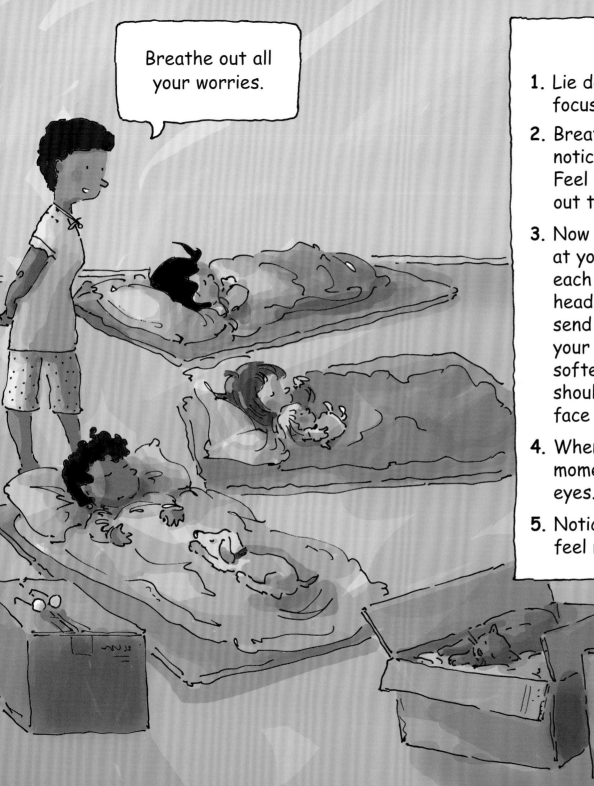

Body Scan

1. Lie down, close your eyes and focus on your breath.

2. Breathe in through your nose, noticing the cool air coming in. Feel the warm air as you breathe out through your mouth.

3. Now focus on your body. Start at your toes and, slowly, with each breath, work up to your head. Each time you breathe in, send that breath to an area of your body, letting it relax and soften. Ask yourself if your shoulders are tight, or if your face is tense.

4. When you are done, rest a few moments before opening your eyes.

5. Notice your whole body. Do you feel relaxed?

Mindful Max

Everybody had a great sleep — except Pedro. He's been using mindfulness exercises but is still worrying about the move. Sally spots Max and has an idea.

With his eyes closed, Pedro really notices the texture of Max's fur. Paying attention to his breath and to his sense of touch helps him feel calm in the moment.

Pets can help us. And not just the cuddly ones! Even paying close attention to fish and snakes can help to bring us into the moment. When you notice your senses, you are more aware of the here and now, and it's hard to worry about the past — or the big move tomorrow!

Be Wise — Visualize!

Pedro waves goodbye to his friends. He is already imagining what it will be like in his new home.

"I hope the move goes well," says Sally.

"I was just thinking the same thing!" says Pedro.

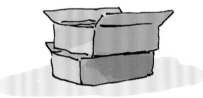

Being mindful is being kind to other people — and to yourself. We all imagine pictures in our heads, some good and some bad. Visualization is using our thoughts to picture something we want. It can be used to reach a goal, send helpful thoughts or feel more comfortable when we decide to try something new.

Mindful Moving!

Look at all the boxes! Pedro has moved into his new house — and he's trying hard to be mindful. He is focusing on unpacking one box at a time and notices that this helps him to feel less anxious.

His friends are at the door, and he can't wait to show them around!

Everyone feels anxious and worried sometimes. Being mindful can give you the tools to help you accept those feelings and not dwell on them. Mindfulness is being aware of what is happening right now — in your surroundings, in your body and in your mind.

Mindful Games

Take a Breath

Fill a jar with water. Rip some paper into tiny pieces and drop them in the water. Put the lid on the jar and shake it up. It's like a snowstorm! This is your mind when you're upset.

Wait a few minutes and watch how the paper floats to the bottom of the jar. Soon the water is clear. This is how our minds work if we take time to breathe. We can see more clearly.

Do Nothing

This is a good way to stop and see how you feel. It's also a reminder that it's okay to just sit and do nothing except notice your breath.

Make it more fun by enjoying a mug of hot chocolate or chamomile tea when you're done. Slowly breathe in the smell. Notice how nice it is to feel your breath coming in through your nose and out through your mouth. Often, when your breath slows down, your body follows.

Eyes of an Eagle

For this game, everybody needs one orange (or any other piece of fruit, as long as they are all the same kind). There should be more oranges than there are players.

Study your orange closely — with the eyes of an eagle! Notice as much as you can, then put it in a basket with all the others. Once all the oranges are returned, mix them up. Can you find your orange again? How did you recognize it?

This game is about really looking and noticing. When you're finished, you can eat your orange. Remember to do it mindfully!

31

Words to Know

body scan: a meditation that helps you become more aware of your body. By paying attention to different parts of your body, from your feet to the muscles in your face, you can identify areas of tension or stress. It can be done while sitting comfortably or lying down with your eyes closed.

focus: to concentrate on one thing, without being distracted by other things

meditation: to focus your thoughts on one thing, like your breath. It's often used to quiet your mind and body.

mindfulness: being aware of this moment, without trying to change it or expect something different

negative thoughts: fear and doubt are examples of negative thoughts

positive thoughts: love and support are examples of positive thoughts

visualization: seeing pictures in your mind. It's often used to help yourself or someone else reach a goal.